FIRST ENCYCLOPEDIA OF AUSTRALIAN Wildlife

Steve Parish

CONTENTS

Glossary
Words included in the glossary are marked with [G]; for example [G]echolocation.

Use of capital letters for animal names in this book
An animal's official common name begins with a capital letter.
Otherwise the name begins with a lower case letter.

Red Kangaroo

Australian animals

Australia and its oceans are home to many fascinating and unusual animals. There are mammals that lay eggs and birds that cannot fly. There are lizards that swim through sand and fishes that walk on their fins. There are even frogs with pockets to carry their babies. All of Australia's amazing animals have bodies and ways of behaving that help them survive.

 **Common Wombat and friends**

Staying alive

Animals need energy to stay alive. They get energy from the food they eat.

Herbivores eat plants.
The Koala is a herbivore.

Carnivores eat animals.
The crocodile is a carnivore.

ᴳOmnivores eat plants and animals.
The Sugar Glider is an omnivore.

ᴳScavengers eat dead animals.
The Tasmanian Devil is a scavenger.

Predators hunt and eat animals.
The spider is a predator.

Prey are hunted and eaten by other animals. The bug is the spider's prey.

Animals need to protect themselves from enemies. Some hide when danger is near. Others have body shapes and colours that make them difficult to see. Some have bodies that are poisonous or too hard to eat. Many animals will fight if they cannot escape. Some defend themselves with fangs, spines or stingers that inject ᴳvenom.

Places to live

An animal's home is called a habitat. It is the place where an animal finds the things it needs to survive. Australia is a very large island with many habitats where different kinds of animals can live.

Types of vegetation

Rainforest

Eucalypt forest

Woodland

Grassland and low trees

Marine Park

Shrubland

Desert

Mountain heath

Coastal swamp forest and heath

Kilometres
0   500   1000

Darwin

Alice Springs

Brisbane

Perth

Adelaide

Sydney

Canberra

Melbourne

Hobart

Seashores

Sea

Wetland

⬆ **Rainforest**

⬆ **Eucalypt forest**

⬆ **Woodland**

⬆ **Shrubland**

⬆ **Grassland**

⬆ **Desert**

⬆ **Mountains**

⬆ **Farmland**

⬆ **Cities**

Mammals

An animal is a mammal if it:

- has a backbone and skull,
- is warm-blooded,
- has lungs and breathes air,
- has hair or fur,
- has two or four limbs, and
- has milk glands.

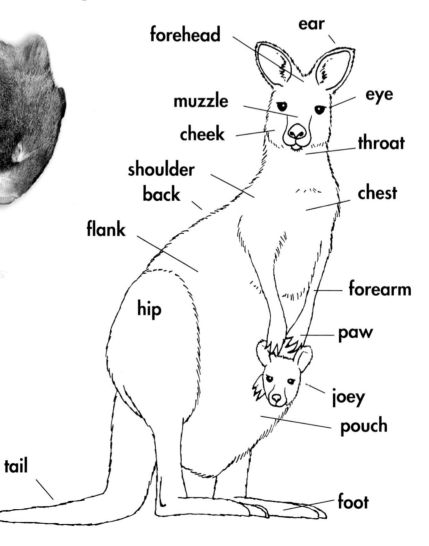

forehead

ear

muzzle

eye

cheek

throat

shoulder
back

chest

flank

forearm

hip

paw

joey

pouch

tail

foot

There are three kinds of mammals:

 Short-beaked Echidna and young

Monotremes (only echidna and platypus) lay soft-shelled eggs. When they hatch, the tiny babies are blind, hairless and have undeveloped back legs. They drink milk that oozes from the skin on the mother's belly.

Northern Quoll newborns

Marsupials (Koala, kangaroo, etc.) give birth to tiny babies that are blind, hairless and have undeveloped back legs. They continue to grow while attached to a nipple in a pouch or fold of skin on the mother's belly.

 Australian Fur-seal pup suckling

Placental mammals (seal, Dingo, etc.) give birth to babies that stay inside the mother's body until they are well developed. After a baby is born, it drinks milk from its mother's nipples (called "suckling").

 **Platypus**

Platypus

Platypuses live in burrows beside creeks and rivers. Thick fur keeps them warm and dry when they hunt for food under water.

A platypus closes its eyes, ears and nostrils when it dives. It catches small animals in its rubbery bill and holds them in its cheeks. It comes to the surface to eat.

Platypuses ^Gmate once a year. The female lays two eggs that hatch in two weeks. She feeds the babies milk until they can look after themselves. The babies are known as puggles, as are baby echidnas.

 **Short-beaked Echidna**

Short-beaked Echidna

The Short-beaked Echidna eats ants and termites. It breaks open their nests with its strong claws. It catches the insects with its long, sticky tongue.

Echidnas live on the ground. They live under thick bushes, in hollow logs or burrows dug by other animals. When an echidna is frightened, it digs into the ground to hide. If the ground is too hard, it rolls up into a spiky ball.

A female echidna lays one egg and carries it in her pouch. The egg hatches in 10 days. The baby, called a puggle, stays in the pouch until its spines grow. Then it is left in a nursery burrow.

▲ **Kultarr**

Marsupial carnivores

Many small marsupials are carnivores – they eat other animals. They are fierce hunters and have sharp teeth. Big eyes help them see at night when they hunt for spiders, insects, birds and other small animals.

Marsupial carnivores sleep during the day. They use leaves and grass to make nests in burrows, logs and tree hollows. Usually, the mothers do not have a pouch. They have folds of skin instead.

Red-cheeked Dunnart

Yellow-footed Antechinus

 **Western Quoll**　　　　　　**Eastern Quoll and kittens** ●›

Quolls

Quolls are cat-sized marsupial ᴳcarnivores. They live on the ground in forest, woodlands and rocky places. These night-time hunters are good climbers. They ᴳprey on insects, lizards, birds and small mammals. Sometimes they eat fruit or dead animals. Quolls are rare animals. Their survival is threatened by tree clearing and ᴳpredators.

▲ **Tasmanian Devil pups playing**　　　　　**Tasmanian Devil** ●▶

Tasmanian Devils

The Tasmanian Devil is Australia's biggest marsupial ᴳcarnivore. It looks fierce, but it is not a good hunter. It is mainly a ᴳscavenger that eats dead animals. It has powerful jaws for crunching bones.

Devils sleep during the day in hollow logs, caves and empty burrows. A mother carries two to four babies in a pouch that faces backwards. When they get too heavy, she leaves them in a nest and brings them food.

 **Numbat**

Numbats

A Numbat is a marsupial that eats termites. It sniffs out underground termites and digs open their trails. It licks up the termites with its long, sticky tongue and swallows them whole.

Numbats sleep at night in hollow branches and logs. They line their nests with leaves and shredded bark.

Numbats are in danger of becoming ^Gextinct. They only live in a small area of forest in Western Australia. Foxes eat them and bush fires destroy their homes.

▲ **Western Barred Bandicoot**

Bandicoots and Bilby

Bandicoots make nests of grass and leaves. They dig up insects, spiders, worms and fungi. They also eat seeds and berries.

The Bilby is a rare bandicoot that lives in the desert. It keeps cool in a deep burrow and eats insects, seeds, bulbs and fungi.

Bandicoots and Bilbies come out to find food at night. Both carry their young in a pouch.

Northern Brown Bandicoot

Bilby

Mother Koala with young one

Koalas

Koalas spend most of their time sleeping. For a few hours each day they eat gum leaves. This food does not give Koalas much energy, so they have to eat a lot to be able to keep warm and move around.

A baby Koala is carried in its mother's pouch where it feeds on her milk. When it is big enough, the joey rides on her back. A Koala may stay with its mother for two years before leaving to find its own home.

 **Northern Hairy-nosed Wombat**

Southern Hairy-nosed Wombat

Common Wombat

Wombats

A wombat is a marsupial. The tiny newborn grows in its mother's pouch. The female's pouch faces backwards so that, when she digs a burrow, dirt does not get inside it. The burrow is a place for sleeping and hiding from enemies.

Wombats have strong front legs and claws for digging. They feed at night on grass and leaves.

There are plenty of Common Wombats in south-eastern Australia. Southern Hairy-nosed Wombats are common but they are found only in small areas of southern Australia. Northern Hairy-nosed Wombats are very rare.

▲ **Female Common Brushtail Possum and baby**

Possums

Possums live in trees. They have sharp claws for holding on tight. Ringtail possums can also hang from their curling tails. Possums come out at night to feed on leaves, sap and fruit. Some possums eat insects.

Possums are marsupials. A newborn baby lives in its mother's pouch feeding on her milk for four to five months. Then the young possum rides on its mother's back until it is big enough to find its own food.

Rock Ringtail Possum and baby

Herbert River Ringtail Possum

Green Ringtail Possum

Striped Possum

Spotted Cuscus

Long-tailed Pygmy-possum

Eastern Pygmy-possum

▲ **Sugar Glider**   **Yellow-bellied Glider** ●➤

Gliders

Gliders are possums – forest marsupials. They feed at night on insects, nectar, leaves and tree sap.

A glider has flaps of skin on each side of its body between the front and back paws. When a glider jumps, it spreads its legs. The flaps of skin act as a parachute, and it glides through the air from tree to tree. Sharp claws help it make a safe landing. It uses its tail for balance when gliding and climbing.

 **Red-necked Wallabies and joey**   **Yellow-footed Rock-wallaby** ●➤

Wallabies

Wallabies are small kangaroos. They have strong back legs and big feet. Most kinds of wallabies live in or near grassy woodlands. They are ᴳherbivores, eating grass and leaves.

Rock-wallabies have special pads on the soles of their feet. This stops them slipping on rocks. They hold their tails high over their bodies for balance when hopping from rock to rock.

▲ **Red Kangaroo holding food in its paws**

▲ **Red Kangaroos**

Kangaroos

Kangaroos are the biggest marsupial mammals in Australia. They live in groups, often called "mobs", led by the strongest males. Kangaroos spend the day resting in shady places. They graze on grass and leaves in the morning and late afternoon.

A baby kangaroo is called a joey. It lives in its mother's pouch until it learns to hop and find its own food.

 **Female Eastern Grey Kangaroo and pouch joey**

 **Black Wallaroo**

 **Common Wallaroo**

 **Diadem Leafnosed-bat**

Spectacled Flying-fox

Northern Blossom-bat

Bats

Bats are the only mammals that can fly. A bat's long fingers are joined to its hind legs by thin skin that forms wings.

To find insects to eat, small bats send out shrill noises. The sounds bounce off flying insects back to the bats. This is called echolocation. Big bats that eat fruit and flowers find food by smell, by sight, and by following noises made by other feeding bats.

▲ **Spinifex Hopping-mouse**

▲ **Brush-tailed Tree-rat**

Rodents

Rats and mice are called rodents. Their sharp front teeth keep growing and never fall out. Rodents gnaw on things to keep their teeth short. They eat seeds, grass, leaves and fruit.

Rodents hide their nests on the ground or in trees. Desert rodents live in burrows and come out at night to feed. Australia has many kinds of native rodents. Different kinds live in different habitats. Some are very rare because foxes and wild cats eat them.

Water-rat

Plains Rat

A Dingo hunting along a beach   Dingos vary in colour

Dingos

The Dingo is a ^Gdescendant of Indian Wolves. People from Asia brought them to Australia thousands of years ago. They became wild and now live in many habitats across Australia.

Dingos are ^Gpredators. They have keen senses of sight, smell and hearing. A Dingo that hunts alone catches small animals. A family of Dingos can chase and catch animals as big as kangaroos.

▲ **Australian Sea-lions** ●▶

Sea-lions

Australian Sea-lions hunt for fishes and squid in cold sea water. They have flippers instead of hands and feet. Dense hair and a thick layer of fat under the skin keep them warm. They are fast and graceful swimmers.

Sea-lions leave the water to ᶜbreed on islands and beaches in southern Australia. A female gives birth to one pup each season. The pup feeds on its mother's milk until it is big enough to swim and catch its food.

▲ **Bottlenose Dolphin**

Dolphins

Dolphins are marine mammals, not fishes. They belong to the same group of animals as whales. They live in groups called pods. A female steers her newborn calf to the surface so it can take its first breath of air.

Dolphins eat fishes and other marine creatures, and they use ᴳecholocation to hunt.

A dolphin swims by using strong muscles to move its tail up and down. It steers with its front flippers.

🔻 **Male Humpback Whale**

Whales

Whales are the largest mammals on Earth. Humpback Whales grow up to 16 metres long and weigh up to 45 tonnes. They feed on ᴳkrill, ᴳplankton and small fishes.

Each winter they swim north from cold Antarctic seas to warm tropical waters to ᴳmate and give birth. A newborn Humpback calf is about 4.3 metres long and weighs about 2.3 tonnes. The males use special songs to send messages to each other on their long journeys.

Birds

An animal is a bird if it:

● has a backbone and a skull,

● is warm-blooded,

● has lungs and breathes air,

● has feathers,

● has one pair of legs, and

● has one pair of wings or flippers.

crown

eye

ear cover

nape

back

bill

throat

breast

rump

abdomen

tail

vent

2

3

4

toe 1

Feathers

A bird must keep its feathers clean and tidy so it can fly. Feathers also keep its body warm and dry.

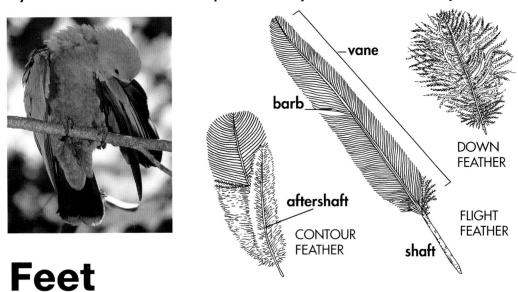

vane

barb

DOWN FEATHER

aftershaft

CONTOUR FEATHER

FLIGHT FEATHER

shaft

Feet

The size and shape of a bird's feet offer many clues about where and how it lives.

emus   *walking*   *swamphens*   *wading*

ducks   *swimming*   *parrots*   *holding*

wrens   *perching*   *owls*   *hunting*

49

 Male Southern Cassowary   **Emu**

Big runners

The Emu and the Southern Cassowary are big, heavy birds. Their wings are small and they cannot fly. They have long, strong legs and can run very fast. They defend themselves by kicking.

Female cassowaries and Emus lay eggs, then the males ᴳincubate them. After the chicks hatch, the males look after them until they are ready to survive on their own. They eat mainly green plants, insects and seeds.

▲ **Malleefowl**

Mound-builders

Some birds keep their eggs warm in huge nests made of leaves and dirt. The male uses his strong feet to build the nest on the ground. The female lays eggs in the nest mound. The male adds and takes away leaves to keep the eggs at just the right temperature.

The chicks hatch inside the nest and dig their way out. They have to look after themselves and can fly soon after hatching.

Australian Brush-turkey

Orange-footed Scrubfowl

🔻 **Black Swan and four cygnets**

🔻 **Freckled Duck**

Waterbirds

Waterbirds with webbed feet are good swimmers. Ducks and swans use their wide beaks to eat water plants and grass seeds.

Birds that wade through the water have long legs and toes. Their toes stop them sinking into the mud. Waders poke about searching for frogs, fishes, worms and small water animals.

Intermediate Egret

Comb-crested Jacana

▲ **Little Penguin – it uses its wings as flippers for swimming**

Seabirds

Seabirds spend most of the day catching fishes. They swallow a lot of salt water when they are fishing. Their bodies use the water and the leftover salt drips out of their nostrils.

Most seabirds have webbed feet. Some float on the water; others swim and dive underwater. They must ᴳpreen often to make sure their feathers don't get waterlogged.

Australian Pelicans

Silver Gull

Masked Boobies

● **Masked Lapwing**

Plains birds

On the plains where there is nowhere to hide, birds use clever tricks to stay alive. Some fly up suddenly from the long grass to surprise and frighten ᶜpredators. Some flap about and pretend to be injured to lead predators away from their nests.

Their best trick is to stay still. Predators have trouble seeing these birds because their colours and patterns blend in with the ground. This is called camouflage.

Australian Bustard

Bush Stone-curlew

 **Tawny Frogmouth**

Night birds

Birds that hunt at night have big eyes that help them to see in the dark, and good hearing. They have soft feathers and can fly very quietly. They also sit quietly and wait patiently for ᴳprey to move across the ground. They eat insects, birds and small animals. During the day, these night-hunters roost in trees.

 **Barking Owl**

Barn Owl

Sooty Owl

▲ **Black-breasted Buzzard with eggs it will break and eat**

Raptors

Raptors are hunting birds. They have powerful legs and feet with sharp claws to catch and hold their ᶢprey. They tear up food with hooked beaks. Raptors have good eyesight.

Eagles and kites soar high above the ground searching for prey. Falcons and hawks can dart between trees and pounce on their prey.

Raptors build nests in tall trees. Some use the same nest every year. They usually have two chicks. Both parents bring food to the babies.

Collared Sparrowhawk

Osprey

▲ **Pair of Rainbow Lorikeets**

Parrots

Parrots are noisy, colourful birds. They have sharp, curved beaks. A parrot's foot has four toes. Two toes point forwards and two point backwards. They use their feet like hands. Parrots build nests in tree hollows.

A big parrot with a crest of feathers on its head is called a cockatoo. Lorikeets, rosellas, cockatiels and budgerigars are small parrots. The members of the parrot family eat seeds, nuts, nectar, flowers, fruit, insects and their ᴳlarvae.

Galahs squabble and play

Crimson Rosellas having a bath

Laughing Kookaburra

Kingfishers

Kingfishers' beaks are long and strong. Kingfishers eat small reptiles, insects, frogs and spiders. Some dive for fishes, and will eat small crabs and yabbies.

Kookaburras are very big kingfishers that live in family groups. When chicks hatch, all the family members help feed them. Kookaburras call loudly to tell other birds that they claim an area as their own.

 **Buff-breasted Paradise-Kingfisher**

Sacred Kingfisher

Forest Kingfisher

▲ **Male Regent Bowerbird**

Bowerbirds

A male bowerbird builds a bower of twigs to attract a ᴳmate. He decorates the bower and sings and dances in front of it. A female picks the male with the best bower. After mating, the female builds a nest where she lays the eggs and looks after the chicks.

Spotted Bowerbird at the entrance to the bower

Satin Bowerbird with decorations for the bower in his beak

Striated Pardalote

Gouldian Finch

Perching birds

A perching bird can curl its feet around a branch when resting. Each foot has three toes pointing forwards and one toe pointing backwards.

These small birds build fancy nests out of grass, twigs, feathers and even spider webs. The whole family looks after the chicks.

Sometimes they are called songbirds because they use complicated songs to communicate with each other. To sing, a bird blows air from its lungs through a vocal °organ called the syrinx.

Blue-faced Honeyeater

Zebra Finch

Rufous Treecreeper

Eastern Yellow Robin

Reptiles

An animal is a reptile if it:

◑ has a backbone and a skull,

◑ is cold-blooded,

◑ has lungs and breathes air,

◑ has dry skin with scales, and

◑ has four limbs (except snakes).

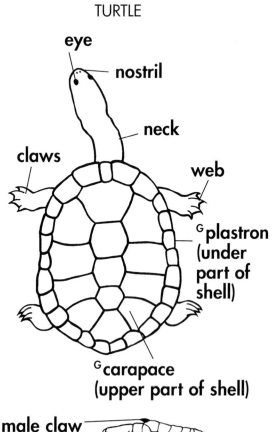

CROCODILES

eye with vertical pupil

nostrils on top of snout

claws

bony plates under skin

vent (under body)

tail sweeps from side to side when swimming

TURTLE

eye

nostril

neck

claws

web

^Gplastron (under part of shell)

^Gcarapace (upper part of shell)

male claw

paddle of marine turtle

🔺 **Lizard (Thorny Devil)**

🔺 **Crocodile (Saltwater Crocodile)**

🔺 **Snake (Carpet Python)**

🔺 **Turtle (Loggerhead Turtle)**

▲ **The Freshwater Crocodile has a narrow snout and thin, sharp teeth**

Crocodiles

Crocodiles live on the coast and in rivers and swamps in northern Australia. They have webbed hind feet and swim by moving their tails from side to side.

Crocodiles hunt at night. Because Saltwater Crocodiles live in salt, ᴳbrackish and fresh water, they are also called Estuarine Crocodiles. They eat anything they can catch. Freshwater Crocodiles ᴳprey on small animals that live in or near the water.

A female crocodile lays her eggs in a nest of dead plants or in sandbanks. She guards her nest until the babies hatch, then she carries them to the water.

▲ **The Saltwater Crocodile has a broad snout and thick, strong teeth**

▲ **Saltwater Crocodiles ^Gbasking**

▲ **Freshwater Crocodiles basking**

🔺 **Brisbane Short-necked Turtles on a log, ^Gbasking**

🔺 **Eastern Snake-necked Turtle**

Freshwater turtles

Most freshwater turtles have webbed feet with claws. Some have flippers instead. They hunt underwater for fishes, frogs, insects and small water animals. They come out of the water to get warm and lay their eggs.

Some turtles walk overland to a new home if their creek or waterhole dries up. Others bury themselves in the mud until it rains.

Krefft's River Turtle

Pig-nosed Turtle

▲ **Green Turtle**

▲ **Flatback Turtle hatchlings**

Sea turtles

Sea turtles are big and heavy. The males never come out of the sea. The females only come onto land to lay their eggs.

A sea turtle swims with its front flippers and steers with the back ones. It must come to the surface to breathe.

Hawksbill Turtle

Flatback Turtle

Small lizards with shiny scales are usually skinks

Closed-litter Rainbow-skink

Skinks

Skinks are lizards that have short, wide tongues and feet with claws. Their bodies are covered by rows of scales. Most skinks, including bluetongues, have smooth shiny scales and pointed tails. Shinglebacks have rough scales and a stumpy tail.

Skinks live in trees, between rocks, under leaves and under the ground. They eat plants and animals.

Shingleback, with short, stumpy tail, bluffing an enemy

Common Bluetongue, with pointed tail

Marbled Velvet Gecko

Geckos

Geckos are soft-skinned lizards. Their fingers and toes end in pads or claws. Each big eye is covered by a see-through goggle. A gecko must lick its eyes to keep them clean.

When an enemy attacks, a gecko can drop its tail and run away. The tail grows again, but has a different pattern on it.

Geckos hunt insects and other small creatures. Some eat other lizards.

Three-lined Knob-tail

Leaf-tailed Gecko

▲ **Two male Perenties wrestling in territorial dispute**

Monitors

Monitors are also called goannas. Perenties are the biggest monitor lizards in Australia. Their rough skins are covered with tiny scales. Strong legs and sharp claws help them run fast and climb trees.

Monitors flick out their forked tongues to taste the air. They can track ᴳprey by the scent the animals leave behind.

Lace Monitor

Gould's Monitor

Merten's Water Monitor

Frilled Lizard raising its frill in alarm

Dragon lizards

Dragon lizards have rough scales. Many have spines on their skin. Some have pouches or frills on their necks to make them look bigger. They can change colour to match their surroundings.

A dragon will run away if its fierce looks and hisses do not frighten an enemy. They move very fast and some stand up to run. They are good tree-climbers.

Most dragon lizards are daytime hunters. They eat insects, small lizards, birds and mammals.

Eastern Water Dragon

Central Netted Ground-dragon

Thorny Devil

Snakes

All snakes are ᴳcarnivores. They have backward-curving, sharp teeth to hold their ᴳprey. Their mouths can move sideways, up and down, and back and forth. Snakes can stretch their jaws very wide. They swallow their food whole instead of chewing it.

Front fangs

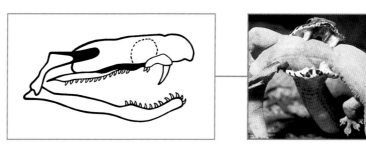

Death Adder

Snakes with hollow front fangs strike quickly and inject their prey with ᴳvenom.

Rear fangs

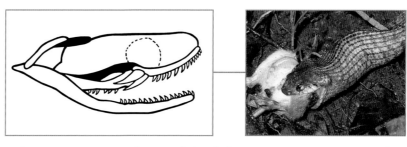

Brown Tree-snake

Rear-fanged snakes must catch and hold their prey before injecting the venom.

No fangs

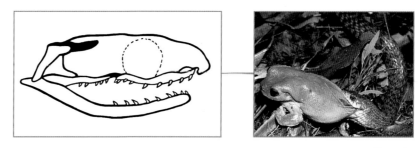

Keelback

Snakes without fangs and venom use their teeth and coils to hold prey while they swallow it.

▲ **Little File Snake**

File snakes

There are only three kinds of file snakes in the world. Two of these live in the coastal wetlands of northern Australia. File snakes have loose skin covered with rough scales with points or ridges. They live in the water and eat fishes. On the land, they move slowly and their bodies are very floppy.

 Green Python

Pythons

Pythons have strong, heavy bodies. Their skin colour can change to ᶜcamouflage their habitat. They have many sharp teeth, but no fangs.

A python coils its body around an animal and squeezes until the animal suffocates. Then the python swallows it whole.

90

Diamond Python

Black-headed Python

🔺 **Green Tree-snake** ◗▸

Tree-snakes

A tree-snake has a long, thin body and a tail like a whip. They are very flexible snakes and some have more than 400 ᴳvertebrae in their spine. They mainly eat frogs and birds that live in trees. Sometimes they hunt for food and water on the ground.

The Brown Tree-snake has short fangs at the back of its mouth. Its ᴳvenom is weak. The Green Tree-snake has solid teeth and no venom.

▲ Eastern Tiger Snake

▲ Lowland Copperhead

Front-fanged snakes

Australia's most dangerous snakes have sharp fangs at the front corners of their top jaws. The fangs stab ᴳprey and inject them with ᴳvenom. Large snakes have very strong venom that kills ᴳprey quickly. Snakes can shed their fangs and grow new ones.

Most front-fanged snakes live and hunt on the ground. They feed on frogs, lizards and small mammals.

Western Brown Snake

Red-bellied Black Snake

Taipan

▲ **Golden (Olive) Seasnake**

Seasnakes

Seasnakes are graceful swimmers. They use their flattened tail as a paddle and ripple their bodies from side to side to move through the water. They can swim backwards and make deep dives. Seasnakes breathe air, but can stay underwater for more than an hour.

Seasnakes are born underwater and most never leave the sea. They have front fangs and very powerful ᴳvenom for killing fishes.

Hydrophis seasnake

Wide-faced Sea Krait

Frogs

An animal is a frog if it:

- has a backbone and a skull,
- is cold-blooded,
- has moist skin with glands, and
- changes shapes during different stages of its life cycle.

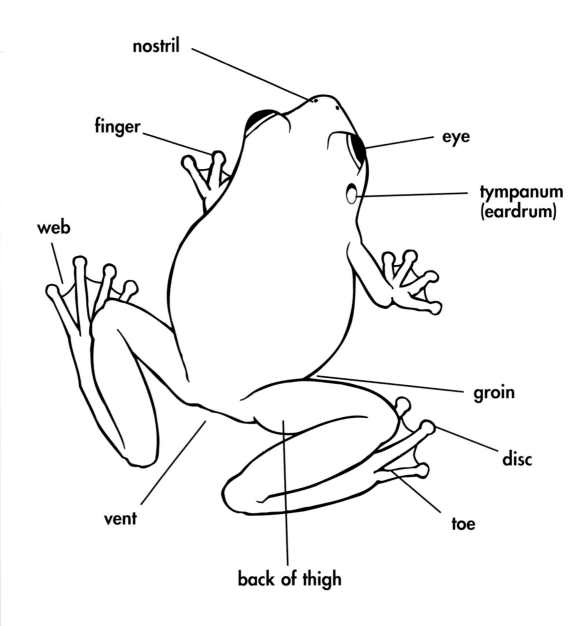

nostril

finger

eye

tympanum (eardrum)

web

groin

disc

vent

toe

back of thigh

A frog's life cycle

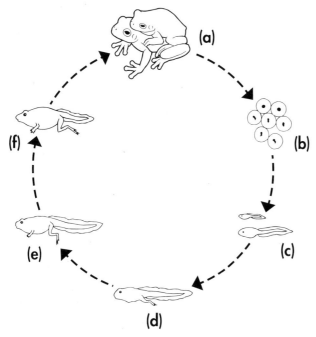

A frog is an amphibian. That means it has two ways of life: in water and on land.

(a) Adult frogs ^Gmate.

(b) Female frog lays eggs.

(c) Tadpoles hatch and grow.

(d-f) Legs and lungs grow, tail shrinks.

A tadpole and an almost grown Striped Marsh Frog tadpole.

A tadpole has ^Ggills, a tail and no legs. Most live in water and eat plants.

Green and Golden Bell Frog

An adult frog has lungs, four legs and no tail. Most frogs live on land. They will eat any animal that will fit in their mouth.

🔺 **Blue Mountains Tree-frog**

Tree-frogs

Most tree-frogs live above the ground in trees and bushes. Round, flat pads on their fingers and webbed toes help them cling to the leaves and branches. Tree-frogs have big eyes for hunting ⁶prey at night.

They lay foamy masses or strings of eggs in water. Fishes and turtles eat frog eggs. Snakes and birds eat frogs. Frogs will eat other frogs.

Green Tree-frogs

Dainty Green Tree-frog

Red-eyed Tree-frog

Moaning Frog producing a creamy substance for protection

Long-footed Frog coming out of its burrow

Burrowing frogs

Frogs that dig burrows have broad heads, round bodies and short legs. Sharp ridges on their back feet help them dig. They sleep underground in dry weather. When it rains, they leave their burrows to look for food and to ᴳmate. The tadpoles of some burrowing frogs change into frogs before they hatch.

Desert Spadefoot Frog's red spots signal it may be poisonous

Water-holding Frog covered in layers of dead skin to keep it moist

Ornate Burrowing Frog

🔺 **Rocket-frog**

🔺 **Northern Gastric-brooding Frog, thought to be ^Gextinct**

Ground frogs

Many kinds of frogs live on the ground. They have long, powerful legs for making quick get-aways. Frogs don't run. They push their back legs straight and leap forward.

Many frogs catch small animals with their sticky tongue. They push large ^Gprey into their mouth with their hands.

Corroboree Frog and eggs with tadpoles inside them

Northern Banjo Frog

Giant Frog eating a smaller frog

Fishes

An animal is a fish if it:

- ●▸ has a backbone and a skull,

- ●▸ is cold-blooded,

- ●▸ has ^Ggills,

- ●▸ has tough skin with scales,

- ●▸ has fins, and

- ●▸ lives in water.

▲ **Freshwater** ^G**habitat**

▲ **Ocean habitat**

Cartilaginous fishes

The ᶜskeleton of a ᶜcartilaginous fish is made of ᶜcartilage.
Cartilaginous fishes include sharks and rays.

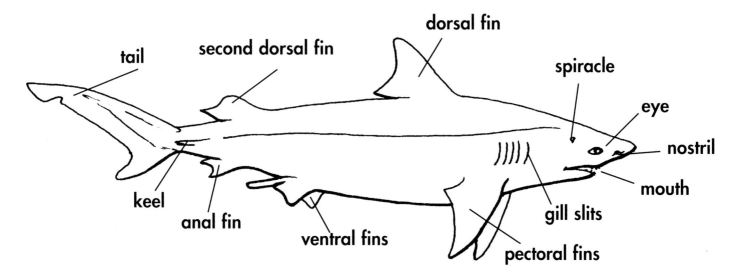

Bony fishes

The skeleton of a bony fish is made of bone.

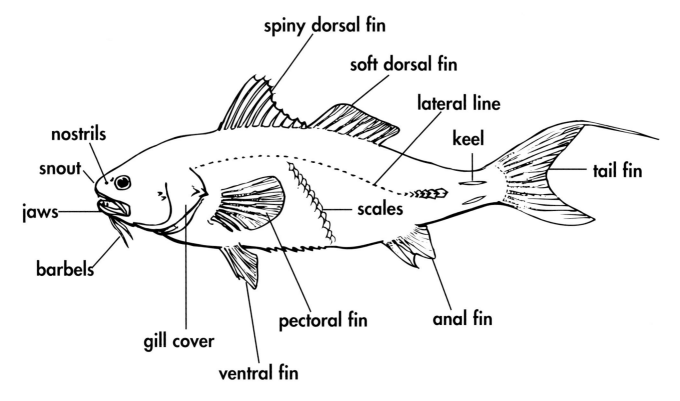

▲ **Whaler Shark**

▲ **Port Jackson Shark**

Sharks

Big, fast-moving sharks travel far to find food. They have powerful jaws and many rows of jagged teeth. They hunt fishes, seabirds and sea mammals, such as dolphins and seals.

Many smaller kinds of sharks have homes. They live around reefs, rocky shores, sandy bays and in river mouths.

Sharks living on the seafloor have ᴳcamouflaged bodies that hide them from ᴳpredators and ᴳprey. They feed on fishes, crabs and ᴳmolluscs.

Whale Shark

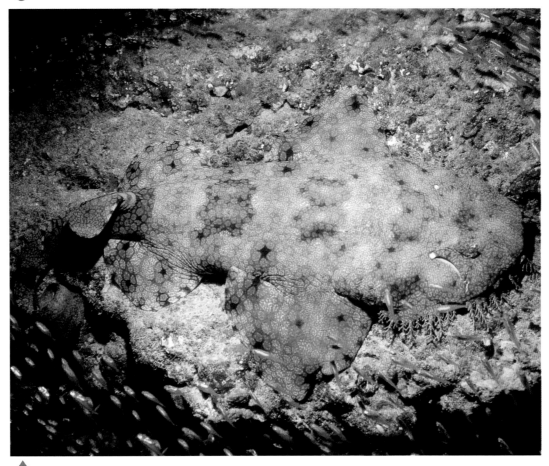

Tasselled Wobbegong

Eastern Fiddler Ray

Rays

A ray's mouth is underneath its flat body. Rays hide on the seafloor ready to pounce on fishes, ᴳmolluscs, and ᴳcrustaceans. Some rays stun their ᴳprey with electric shocks. Many rays have a spine that carries ᴳvenom on their tail.

The giant Manta Ray lives near the surface. It swims with its mouth wide open to catch ᴳplankton.

Eastern Shovelnose Ray

Common Stingaree

Manta Ray

Green Moray Eel

Trumpetfish

Strange fishes

Not all fishes look like fishes. Some can look like rocks, seaweed or other kinds of animals. But they all have fins and ᴳgills, and only fishes have those.

Fishes have to compete with thousands of sea animals for food and homes. Having a strange shape can help a fish to find a safe place to live and things to eat that no other animals want.

▲ **Weedy Seadragon**

▲ **Thorny-back Cowfish**

▲ **Big-eye Trevally**

▲ **A school of hardyheads**

Open ocean fishes

There is no place to hide in the open ocean. Fishes must swim fast to escape enemies. Many fishes swim in large groups called schools. A ᴳpredator can be tricked by a school of small fishes because, when it moves, it looks like one big fish.

Fishes that live in the open sea are darker coloured on their back and lighter on their belly. This colour pattern makes them hard to see from above and from below.

▲ Southern Spiny Gurnard

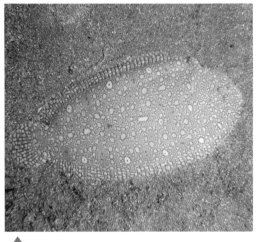

▲ Peacock Sole

▲ Stargazer

Seafloor fishes

Fishes that live on the seafloor usually have a flat belly, a wide mouth and eyes on top of the head. Their colour and shape act as ^Gcamouflage. They are patient hunters that wait and watch for ^Gprey to come close.

Some use their side fins to hop along the bottom or to prop themselves up. Others use their fins like wings to glide short distances. Many seafloor fishes hide under sand, mud or seaweed.

 Emperor Angelfish

Moorish Idol

Reef fishes

Rocky and coral reefs are home to many fishes. Small or thin fishes can dart in and out of tiny holes and narrow crevices. Bigger fishes swim over and around the reefs, resting under ledges and in caves.

Tropical reef fishes have bright colours and bold patterns to blend in with the coral. Rocky reef fishes have colours and shapes that match the rocks and seaweed.

Pink Anemonefish

Harlequin Tuskfish

⬥ **Chinaman Leatherjackets attacking a seahorse**

Fishes on rocky reefs

Around the south of Australia, the water is too cold for coral to grow. These coasts have rocky platforms and reefs. The waves on rocky coasts are often rough.

Some fishes can live where the water rushes over rock platforms. Others live further out to sea where there are plenty of rock caves and cracks for shelter.

Pineapplefish

Golden Weedfish

▲ Barramundi live in fresh water, and ^Gbreed in salty water

▲ Striped Scat

Freshwater fishes

Freshwater fishes and their eggs are food for animals that live on land and in the water.

Fishes can hide from ^Gpredators, but it is hard to keep their eggs safe. Some keep their eggs in their mouth until they hatch. Others have eggs that stick to plants and are not easy to see.

Some fishes grow up in fresh water, then move to salty water to ^Gmate and lay their eggs.

Western Rainbowfish

Firetail Gudgeon

Olive Perchlet

Insects

An animal is an insect if it:

●▶ has a ᴳskeleton on the outside of its body,

●▶ has a head, thorax and abdomen,

●▶ has 3 pairs of walking legs,

●▶ has 1 pair of ᴳantennae,

●▶ has jaws, and

●▶ lays eggs.

Most insects have wings and change shape during different stages of their life cycles.

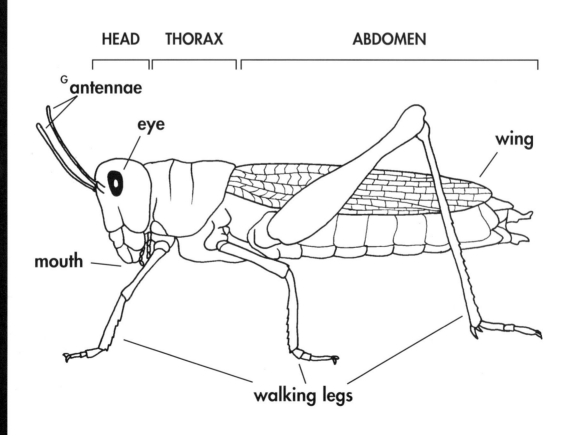

HEAD   THORAX   ABDOMEN

ᴳantennae

eye

wing

mouth

walking legs

Insect life cycles

No change

[G]Primitive insects look like small adults when they hatch. They just grow bigger as they get older. These insects do not have wings.

Silverfish keeps its shape

Gradual changes

Some insects change shape gradually as they grow. Their wings sprout and grow.

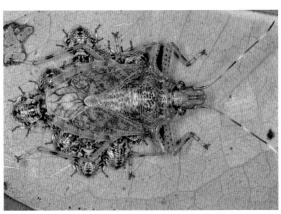

Young bugs change gradually

Big changes

An insect's egg hatches into a [G]larva – a caterpillar or grub. It grows, then turns into a pupa which lives in a case of hard skin called a chrysalis. During this resting stage, the pupa grows wings and becomes an adult.

Butterfly larva, or grub

Butterfly pupal case, or chrysalis

Adult Lemon Migrant Butterfly

▲ Meat Ants

▲ Green Ant

Ants and termites

Ants and termites live in big families called colonies. A
^Gcolony has a queen, her ^Gmates and thousands of
workers and soldiers.

An ant egg hatches into a grub with no legs or
^Gantennae. The grub grows, then changes into an
adult. When termites hatch they look almost like
adults. As they grow they look more like their parents.

Ants and termites are nature's recyclers. They clean
up the ground, and the wastes from the plants and
animals they eat are good for the soil.

Termite mound and Frilled Lizard

Harvester Termites

▲ **Leichhardt's Grasshopper**

Grasshoppers

Grasshoppers, crickets, katydids and locusts all belong to the same group of insects. They use their springy hind legs to launch themselves into the air. They have two pairs of wings, but are not good fliers.

Grasshoppers live near the ground and eat grass and other plants. Crickets and katydids live in trees, on the ground and in burrows. They feed on plants and other insects. Locusts are strong fliers that travel far in big groups called swarms.

 Short-horned grasshopper

 Leopard Grasshopper

 Sandstone Grasshopper

▲ A Dawson's Burrowing Bee peers from its nest burrow

▲ A social burrowing bee gathering nectar

Bees and wasps

Only a few native bees and wasps live in colonies. [G]Introduced Honey Bees live together in a hive, but most bees live alone. The females lay eggs in burrows. They put pollen and nectar in the burrows for the [G]larvae to eat.

Many wasps lay their eggs on or in living plants and animals. When they hatch, the larvae eat their live nests.

Adult bees and wasps carry pollen from flower to flower when they feed on nectar. This helps flowers make seeds so new plants can grow.

Mud-dauber Wasp carrying a paralysed caterpillar to her nest

Paper-nest Wasp and nest cells

▲ **Ladybirds**

Bugs and beetles

A bug stabs its sharp beak into a plant or animal, then sucks up the juices. A beetle chews its food with jaws that move sideways.

A bug hatches from an egg and gradually grows into an adult. A beetle's body changes shape as it grows. It changes from an egg into a grub and then into an adult.

Stag beetle

Assassin bug

Stink bug

▲ **Zodiac Moth**

▲ **Whistling Moth**

Moths and butterflies

Many moths, butterflies and their caterpillars are colourful. Bright colours on bodies and wings warn ᶜpredators that these creatures may be poisonous or taste terrible.

A moth's back wings hook onto the front ones so the wings beat at the same time. It folds its wings beside its body to rest. A butterfly's wings do not hook together. It rests with its wings folded above its body.

Red Lacewing Butterfly

Leafwing Butterfly

Underside of a Cruiser Butterfly

Spiders

An animal is a spider if it:

- ⬤❯ has a ᴳskeleton over part of its body,
- ⬤❯ has a head and an abdomen,
- has 4 pairs of walking legs,
- ⬤❯ does not have ᴳantennae,
- ⬤❯ does not have wings,
- ⬤❯ has silk glands,
- ⬤❯ has fangs that inject ᴳvenom, and
- ⬤❯ lays eggs.

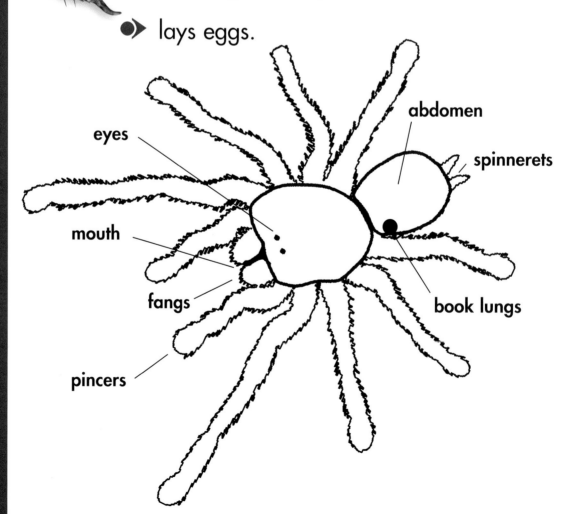

eyes

abdomen

spinnerets

mouth

fangs

pincers

book lungs

Silk spinners

Spiders are expert spinners and weavers. They make silk inside their body, then spin it into strong thread. They weave the threads into shelters, burrow linings and egg sacs. Spiders also make an amazing variety of traps to catch ᶜprey. They weave trip-wires, throwing nets, lures and sticky webs.

Building an orb web

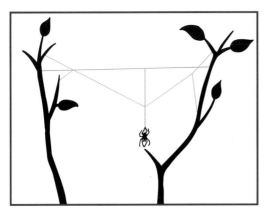

1. The spider attaches a thread between two branches. Then it makes three spokes in a Y shape.

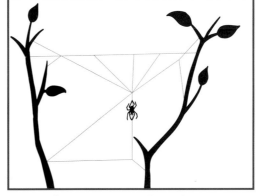

2. A frame is made. Then more threads are attached to leaves and branches.

3. The web is finished with sticky thread that goes around in a spiral starting from the centre.

4. Spiders have bristly hairs on their feet so they don't stick to their own webs.

🔻 **Trapdoor spider**

Primitive spiders

A ᶜprimitive spider is a lot like its ᶜprehistoric ᶜancestors. It lives in a burrow or tube of silk. It has a big, hairy body. Its jaws move up and down and have fangs that inject ᶜvenom. It also has eight eyes on top of its head. A primitive spider breathes through lungs that look like ᶜgills. There is one of these book-lungs on each side of its body.

Trapdoor and Funnel-web spiders are the biggest and most ᶜvenomous spiders in Australia.

Wolf spider

Huntsman spider with katydid

▲ Redback Spider

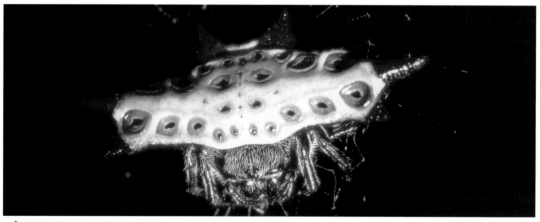

▲ Jewel Spider

Modern spiders

ᴳModern spiders have bodies of all shapes and sizes. Their jaws move sideways and they have ᴳvenomous fangs. They breathe through book-lungs and an air tube. Modern spiders have six or eight eyes. These spiders are experts at spinning and weaving silk. They use it for building shelters, wrapping up their eggs and trapping ᴳprey.

138

▲ **Net-casting spider**

▲ **St Andrews Cross Spider**

Marine invertebrates

Marine ^{G}invertebrates are animals that live in the sea and that do not have a backbone. They have bodies of all shapes, sizes and colours. Many are attached to the bottom, and look more like plants or rocks than animals. Most sea creatures live in shallow water where there is plenty of food. But there is not a lot of space for so many animals. They crowd together and live on, under and even inside each other.

The ocean is home to many kinds of life forms

▲ **Sponge**

Sponges

Baby sponge animals float in the sea, then attach themselves to the bottom and grow. A sponge eats by sucking in water through small holes in its body. It strains plankton – tiny animals and plants – out of the water and eats them. Then it pumps the water out through a large hole.

▲ **Sea-jellies have stinging tentacles**

Sea-jellies

A sea-jelly has a hollow body shaped like a dome or a box. Its mouth is underneath its body. Tentacles with stingers surround the mouth. The tentacles catch ᴳplankton and small fishes and push them towards the sea-jelly's mouth.

Sea turtles and some fishes eat sea-jellies.

142

Mosaic Sea-jellies

Lion's Mane Sea-jelly

 Feeding tentacles of polyps of Sunshine Coral   Soft coral

Corals

A coral animal is called a polyp. Some build hard ᴳskeletons around their bodies. Hard corals that live in colonies need clean, warm water to grow into reefs. Soft coral polyps live in a ᴳcolony and their bodies are connected. The colony has a fragile skeleton of crystals. Coral polyps feed on ᴳplankton they catch with their tentacles.

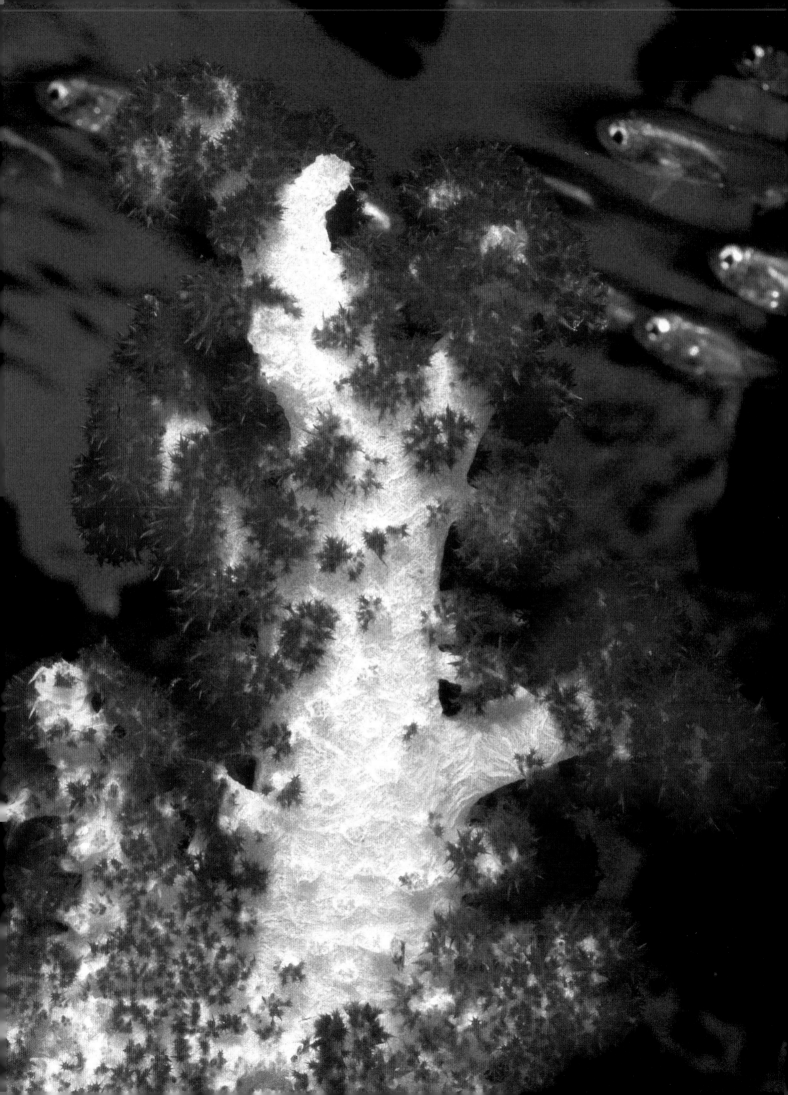

Sea anemone

Anemones

An anemone has a mouth surrounded by stinging tentacles on top of its body. It can pull in its tentacles and squash up its body to escape ^Gpredators. It uses a sucker on the end of its body to creep and climb.

Christmas Tree Worm

Bristle worm

Worms

There are all kinds of worms in the sea. Flat ones ripple their body through the water. Long ones with bristly legs crawl around snapping up small sea creatures. Some bore tunnels into rock and coral. Others live in tubes they build in sand, coral or on rocks.

▲ **Painted Cray**

Crustaceans

Crabs, crays, shrimps and prawns protect their soft bodies with hard, outside ᴳskeletons. They have ten legs and two ᴳantennae. Their eyes are on stalks because they cannot turn their heads. A ᴳcrustacean has to shed its skeleton each time it grows. It hides in a safe place until the new skeleton becomes hard.

⬥ **Soldier Crab**

⬥ **Burrowing shrimp**

⬥ **Hermit Crab**

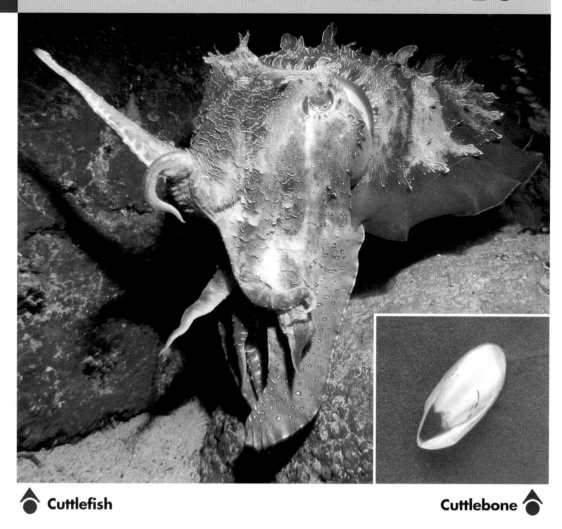

▲ Cuttlefish

Cuttlebone ▲

Molluscs with shells

A mollusc's soft body is covered by special skin called a mantle that makes its shell.

A mollusc with one shell has a head and one muscular foot. It has a raspy tongue that scrapes off food or drills into other animals. A mollusc with two shells has no head. Its ᴳgills sieve food out of the water.

Squid and cuttles are molluscs with a small shell inside their body. Ten tentacles with suckers surround their mouth.

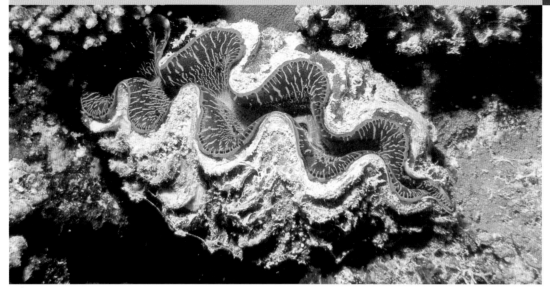

▲ **Giant Clam**

▲ **Textile Cone**

▲ **Squid**

▲ **Nudibranch**

Molluscs without shells

Octopuses and nudibranchs (say *nudi-branks*) are molluscs that have no shell. An octopus has a beak like a parrot's. Its mouth is surrounded by eight tentacles.

Most nudibranchs have feathery ᴳgills on their backs but some have bumps like warts. Nudibranchs look like brightly coloured slugs.

Octopus

Nudibranch

▲ **Feather star**

Sea stars

Sea stars have tiny, hollow feet on their arms. They pump water through these tube-feet to make them move. As brittle stars and ordinary sea stars walk over the bottom, they hunt for small animals to eat. A feather star waves its arms around to catch ᵍplankton. Its tube-feet pass the food to its mouth. If a sea star breaks an arm, it can grow a new one.

Sea star

Brittle star

A live sea urchin hides under the shell of a dead one

Sea urchins

A sea urchin's body is covered with sharp spines. Some urchins can inject ᴳvenom through their spines. They use their bottom spines and tube-feet for walking.

An urchin's mouth is under its body. It has jaws with teeth for scraping up seaweed and sponges.

156

▲ **Sea cucumber with tentacles extended**

Sea cucumbers

A sea cucumber has a long body with leathery skin and no arms. Most crawl over the bottom on three rows of tube-feet.

Tentacles around the mouth catch ᴳplankton and small animals. Some sea cucumbers plough along the bottom, gobbling up lots of sand or mud with their food.

People and wildlife

You can learn a lot about how animals live and behave by watching them in their habitats.

▲ **Binoculars are handy for watching birds**

Make notes and drawings 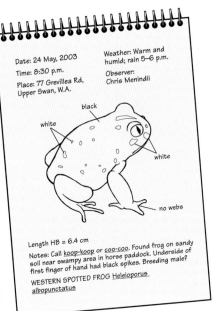 about the animals you see. Then use animal books to help you find out their names.

Date: 24 May, 2003
Time: 8:30 p.m.
Place: 77 Grevillea Rd, Upper Swan, W.A.

Weather: Warm and humid; rain 5–6 p.m.
Observer: Chris Menindii

black
white
white
no webs

Length HB = 6.4 cm
Notes: Call koop-koop or coo-coo. Found frog on sandy soil near swampy area in horse paddock. Underside of first finger of hand had black spikes. Breeding male?
WESTERN SPOTTED FROG Heleioporus albopunctatus

What to look for

Size: Compare to an animal you know.
Shape: Of body parts.
Colour: Of body parts.
Call: Describe the animal's voice.
Behaviour: Describe what the animal is doing.
Habitat: Describe where the animal lives.

Be aware

Some Australian animals have bites and stings that can harm people. Very few wild animals deliberately attack people, but a frightened or confused animal will defend itself. Most injuries happen by accident or when people try to catch or kill animals.

▲ **Land clearing may destroy animal habitats**

▲ **Old trees are animal homes**

▲ **Learning about our native animals helps protect them**

▲ **Feral cats ᴳprey on Australian animals**

Wildlife conservation

Animals can become ᴳextinct if their habitats change too much. If they cannot find the food and protection they need, they cannot stay alive to ᴳmate and have babies.

When humans change the natural environment to make their own habitats, they can damage or destroy wildlife habitats. By looking after Australia, its oceans, plants and animals, we help keep the Earth a clean and healthy place for all living things.

Glossary

ancestor A relative from many hundreds or thousands of years ago.

antennae Feelers.

basking Lying in a sunny place.

brackish *Brackish* water is water that is a mixture of fresh and salt water.

breed To have young ones that can also have their own young.

camouflage Colouring that helps an animal blend with its background.

carapace A hard shell covering the top and sides of an animal's body.

carnivore An animal that eats other animals.

cartilage (noun) Gristle.

cartilaginous (adjective) Having a skeleton of cartilage.

crustacean A shellfish, such as a prawn or crab.

colony A group of the same kind of animals living together.

descendant A relative of an ancestor.

echolocation The use of high-pitched sounds and echoes to find objects.

extinct Having no living examples of the same kind.

gills Breathing organs for animals that live in water.

herbivore An animal that eats plants.

incubate To keep eggs at the right temperature for hatching live young.

introduced (When we talk about an animal or plant) brought from the country it originally came from to another country.

invertebrate An animal that has no backbone.

krill Small shrimps that are found together in large numbers.

larva (singular) The grub or caterpillar that hatches from a butterfly or moth egg. **larvae** (plural) More than one larva.

mate When animals *mate* (*verb*), the male transfers special cells to the female's eggs that cause young ones to develop. An animal's *mate* (*noun*) is the partner with which it has young ones.

modern (When we talk about spiders) different from the very first of their kind in some body parts and ways of living.

mollusc An invertebrate with a soft body and, usually, a shell. Molluscs can be very small, or as big as the giant clam.

omnivore An animal that eats plants and other animals.

organ A very important body part, such as the heart or lungs, that does a particular job to help an animal live.

plankton Very tiny plants and animals that drift in water.

plastron The shell covering the underside of the body of a tortoise or turtle.

predator An animal that hunts and eats other animals.

preen When a bird *preens*, it uses its beak to keep its feathers clean and neat.

prehistoric From a time many thousands of years ago.

prey (noun) An animal hunted and eaten by other animals. (verb) to hunt and eat animals.

primitive Not much changed from the very first of its kind, many thousands of years ago.

scavenger An animal that eats dead animals.

skeleton The hard material, such as bones or a shell, of a living thing's body.

venom (noun) Poison made by animals that is injected by fangs, spines or stingers. **venomous** (adjective) Having venom.

vertebrae More than one of the bones in a backbone or spine.

Index